Common Threads Playwork Classics Series

Adventure Playgrounds
A Progress Report

National Playing Fields Association
(now Fields In Trust)

Second Edition

www.commonthreads.org.uk

ISBN: 978-1-904-79235-2

COMMON THREADS PLAYWORK CLASSICS SERIES
Series Editor: Shelly Newstead

Adventure Playgrounds – A Progress Report Second Edition

© Fields In Trust

First Edition published 1960 by National Playing Fields Association (now Fields In Trust www.fieldsintrust.org)

The right of the Fields In Trust to be identified as the author of this work has been asserted by them in accordance with sections 77 and 78 of the Copyright, Designs and Patents Act 1988.

All efforts have been made to trace the copyright holders for this work. In the event of any queries, please contact the publishers as below.

This document is an original document and reflects the legislation and policy of its time. It should not be used as a guide to current legislation or policy. Up-to-date information should be sought regarding current legal and good practice requirements.

Printed in the UK by Lightning Source UK Ltd.

All rights reserved. No part of this publication may be produced in any form or by any means, without prior permission of the publisher.

British Library Cataloguing in Publication Data
A catalogue record for this book is available from the British Library.

Common Threads Publications Ltd
Wessex House
Upper Market Street
Eastleigh, Hampshire
SO50 9FD UK
E: info@commonthreads.org.uk
W: www.commonthreads.org.uk

Registered Company Number 4500413.

ADVENTURE PLAYGROUNDS

INTRODUCTION

IN 1952 the Children's Playground Committee of the National Playing Fields Association decided that grants should be given to the proposed adventure playgrounds in Lollard Street at Lambeth and Rathbone Street, Liverpool. As these playgrounds were to be of an experimental nature it was further decided that they should have rather favoured treatment to try to get them on their feet so that an assessment might be made of the value of this type of playground.

Since then much has been learnt about adventure playgrounds and a number of others have come into existence. It very soon became apparent that the overriding factor in making a success of any one of the playgrounds lay in the person of the play leader. Site, equipment and even finance (apart from the provision of the leader's salary) fall into insignificance in comparison with the importance of the personality of the play leader. The second major factor, also linked with the person of the play leader, was the continuity of his tenure of office and the regularity of his attendance at the playground.

With the shortage of trained personnel and the difficulty of finding suitable people to take over this type of work the playgrounds have gone through a series of vicissitudes. Moreover the playgrounds have developed in different directions owing to the influence of the play leaders and the facilities available. For both these reasons it would be unwise at the moment to make specific recommendations about the methods and practice of their running and administration but while that may be difficult there is no doubt whatsoever that the playgrounds are serving a most useful purpose and where the problem of getting the right play leader has been settled the parents and authorities in the neighbourhood seem well pleased with the results.

The National Playing Fields Association decided to produce this brochure giving details about the administration, financing and running of Adventure Playgrounds with a short summary of the activities which take place in six individual playgrounds as a guide for those who contemplate starting a playground of this type.

Cover Photograph by courtesy of 'The Grimsby Evening Telegraph'

LOLLARD ADVENTURE PLAYGROUND

The Lollard Adventure Playground lies just across the river from the Houses of Parliament, between the Lambeth Walk and the Kennington Road. It is surrounded by small streets of old houses, many of them condemned before the war, where a large proportion of the wage-earners are manual workers. At a little distance, modern blocks of flats have replaced the old property and the whole of the immediate area, including the playground site of 1¼ acres, will make way for a new school within the next few years. Then the experiment on this site will come to an end.

Meanwhile, it is still growing and changing, as it has done in the past. This spring (1960) it will be five years old. At first, it was regarded as a wild-cat scheme, unlikely to live. "It's just one of those things," said a neighbour, "a flash in the pan." Now it is an established feature of the neighbourhood and a centre where visitors from all over the world find something to learn. In the informal, outdoor setting, with a resourceful, sympathetic warden, and equipment and materials that lend themselves to endless adaptation, the children are enjoying a unique range of pleasures and interests and responsibilities.

PAST AND PRESENT

In the autumn of 1954 the present Chairman and the founder members of the Lollard Adventure Playground Association in co-operation with the N.P.F.A. successfully negotiated with the Education Committee of the L.C.C. for the use of a bombed school site in Lollard Street. This was a bold step, since at that time, in spite of a few pilot experiments and a three-year propaganda campaign, public opinion still favoured the hard-surface, swing-and-see-saw playgrounds which had been a standard feature, all over the country, as long as anyone could remember. "What more can the children want?" was a question that was asked in all seriousness.

The sponsors of the Lollard scheme took a different view. The well-equipped playgrounds were attracting some of the children, some of the time ; but what was being done for the children who preferred to go off and play on the bomb-sites? A playground which would give them a comparable sense of adventure did not need expensive fixtures. It must provide opportunities—tools, materials, rough ground and the friendship and backing of a friendly, skilful supervisor.

On this basis, the Lollard Adventure Playground Association on which local interests, the Borough Council, the County Council and the N.P.F.A. were represented was formed. Money was raised from various sources and special credit is due to the grant-giving bodies who showed their faith in the experiment, at this early stage, by guaranteeing the essentials :—

The London County Council leased the site at a nominal rent and gave the surround fencing. Since 1956 they have given an annual grant corresponding to the warden's salary.

The Borough of Lambeth surfaced the ball-games area and undertook to maintain it. Later, an annual grant was voted, now standing at £200.

The National Playing Fields Association gave £800 to cover the warden's salary for the first 18 months, and have since given more help on a number of critical occasions.

The London and Greater London Playing Fields Association gave £800 towards capital cost—lavatories, water supply, shelters, etc.

From these sources, too, the committee received much wise counsel on the general conduct of affairs, legal and technical advice and secretarial services. The value of such support can hardly be over-estimated. A successful voluntary committee represents, in any case, a great deal of hard work done by individual members in their spare time ; and much energy and good-will is wasted if the business is not conducted with speed and efficiency.

The committee appointed a warden and opened the playground in the Easter holidays of 1955. It still looked like a bomb-site, with old foundations outcropping through the dusty earth and a top-dressing of rubbish. The surround fence was not yet up. The warden's only shelter, for bad days, was a roadman's hut. The materials provided for the children's use disappeared mysteriously, on bonfires and elsewhere : and the neighbours had not got out of the habit of dumping rubbish as soon as one lot was cleared up.

But children of all ages came in—sometimes, if Mum was busy, bringing " their babies " too. There were no formalities, nothing to pay, no restrictions about wandering in and out. It was a place where they could dream or potter, or let off steam in their own way, with full adult approval. " In the streets," says one girl, " you were *always* in trouble—for making a noise, waking the baby, things like that." Here there was nothing, within the limits of safety, that was not allowed. Bonfires, for instance, were so popular that the number alight at one time had to be limited to six ; and later, for the sake of the neighbours, Monday washday was declared a close season.

The reaction of the neighbourhood was mixed. " Look at them, teaching the children to destroy things," said one passer-by. But her friend took a broader view. " Well, it's an *adventure* playground. We ought to be thankful that there *is* a place where they *can* destroy things."

Some parents, meanwhile, were pleased that something had been done for their children, but they did wish they didn't get so dirty. The older people didn't care for it. " We didn't have it, why should they have it ? This sort of thing we never had, it can't do any good." In general, the place was regarded as " an eyesore." It was called " The Ruins," " The Junk Heap," " Crazy Court " and other names which are not printable.

Heavy rains that year made things particularly difficult, yet gradually the playground improved. The hard-surface area was ready for the children to play on when the main playground was closed. The fencing was completed. A large hut, acquired at a cut rate, was erected at considerable cost ; and a corner was marked out alongside for the younger children, with a sandpit designed and built by the older ones. Other additions were books for a library, more building materials, a grounded lifeboat and an old van which turned out to be mobile. Money was always needed, and was raised from many sources—ranging from half-crown subscriptions to £650 from The Variety Club of Great Britain.

The playground still qualified as an eyesore but the children themselves brought into it life and colour—some of them playing explorers on the boat, some digging, some reading, some building camps for themselves and some helping with clearance or mixing and laying cement.

There were a few disappointments. The first planting, by a garden contractor, was a failure ; and the free-and-easy outdoor style of the summer months was not suited to the winter. Painting and modelling sessions were a success with some children but unorganised groups were apt to interfere with each other inside the hut while the warden was trying, vainly, to keep an eye on those who had stayed outside.

This was a mistake which could be, and has been, corrected. Another mistake was made the following summer when the committee, planning to make the flat site more interesting, accepted an offer of " topsoil " to make an artificial mountain. The children seized the opportunity for " terrific games, inspired probably by current films, with rushes of movement across the place, all ages, with others tagging on behind." But their pleasure was brief. The promised topsoil turned out to be London clay and there was an outcry from parents who found it trodden all over their well-kept homes. All efforts to control it by retaining walls, or planting, proved futile ; and it finally had to be carted away, at great expense.

This is an episode that is vividly remembered. " When the mountain was brought in, people were standing there jeering, ' What do they think they are doing? ' Then more jeering when it was taken away."

Throughout this period, local committee members were continually waylaid by destructive critics and the warden, a visible target, was under almost constant fire. Even when nothing was said, he sensed disapproval. " I feel them looking at me out of all those little houses." He had worked nobly through the first heat of the day, with no deputy warden and only a sketchy team of voluntary helpers, but at this point he resigned.

The Committee, after a few weeks of doubt and difficulty, appointed the present warden. Later, the staff was increased. The Halley Stewart Trust gave a grant for the salary of an assistant, and the Save the Children Fund sponsored an under-fives group, with experienced staff paid directly by them.

These were big improvements. The playground has been used since, during school hours, by the under-fives ; and the warden's task has become less lonely and exacting. He has more time free from general supervision for collecting material, initiating new products, making local contacts and enlisting voluntary help. Attendances have gone up. In the summer of 1958, there were occasions when 250 children were on the playground at one time. All age-groups are still well represented and a new one has been added—the boys and young men who "join the workshop." The oldest is 23, and most of those who are over 16 are at work.

The workshop, the Old Age Pensioners' scheme and the magazine are permanent, year-round interests. In the summer, camping, hut-building and gardening are obvious attractions, varied by bursts of enthusiasm for cricket, bumble-puppy, target tennis and the interesting new games taught by a Swedish visitor, while winter activities include painting, modelling, jiving and " beauty " sessions for the girls.

The programme, in any case informal, is varied by parties, treats and money-raising efforts in which the children play a part. Among the special occasions of 1958 were a Christmas party given to the Old Age Pensioners, a Jumble Sale which raised £24 and a puppet show given by post-graduate students from Maria Grey College. This is now an annual event and the students feel that their "efforts are richly rewarded by the radiant attention of the children."

Outside contacts also contribute to the variety and vigour of the playground. Visitors come often and the children are now seasoned hosts, very ready with a friendly greeting and any help that is wanted ; and equally capable of keeping on, undisturbed, at their own affairs. Students, and others concerned with children, have appreciated this opportunity ; and the press, radio and television have made good use of the material that has been given them. Articles, letters and comment have appeared in the local and the national press ; the chairman, the warden, and a number of children have appeared on T.V. ; and paintings done by the children were shown in the B.B.C. " Monitor " programme " The Innocent Eye."

This represents a real contribution to public understanding of adventure playgrounds. In addition, local good will, already responsive to the sight of a good garden, and to the knowledge that the children are working hard to do something for the Old Age Pensioners, is strengthened by the appearance of " our playground " on television.

In spite of all this publicity, a legend still persists that the playground is provided, out of public money, by THEM, and it is worth emphasising again that the Association is a voluntary body, depending on the efforts of private people. The treasurer comments " The major part of our initial experiment and the whole cost of salaries is met by generous grants from the sources already named. But the routine administration and maintenance charges are rarely less than £400 a year, £200 of which is generously donated by the Lambeth Borough Council. The remainder has to be met by donations, subscriptions and special activities. Necessary improvements to the playground are not covered by the routine charges. Some represent extra expenditure ; others are the result of generous gifts of materials."

The playground has many facets and, like all good Adventure Playgrounds, is in a continual process of destruction and growth. It is this capacity for development that marks it out from the more static type of playground of asphalt and mechanical swings. It differs too in its wide age range. Most playgrounds stand empty for a large part of the year—a waste of valuable space and opportunity. They are unused while the children are at school and are usually closed at dusk. The Lollard Playground is extensively used by children under five years of age when their older brothers and sisters are at school. Since the war the Government have insisted on a total ban on all new open-air nursery schools—perhaps the ideal setting for small children who live in the crowded urban areas. These little children are too often denied opportunities for play in safe and secure surroundings during their formative years. Usually living in small flats where opportunities for play and for making a noise are severely limited, they have only the streets to play in. In the Lollard Adventure Playground they have freedom, space and a chance to experiment with water, earth and other materials. Their mothers are relaxed and grateful, for they know their children are cared for with affection and understanding.

In those orthodox playgrounds which have mechanical equipment no child under five is admitted unless in charge of an adult and the facilities for free, experimental play are usually absent. At the other end of the age range, most playgrounds are closed to children over fourteen years and even for those under this age there is very little to captivate their imagination. Children and young people up to eighteen years and over (and of course their parents) are welcome at the Lollard Adventure Playground and they come because they find personal warmth and understanding.

It is the fashion these days to establish coffee-and-jive clubs to keep growing adolescents off the street with the emphasis that there must be no " do-them-good " atmosphere. In a recent article in *The Times* it was written that growing boys and girls " must not be called upon to use their brains " and they " must not be asked for anything in return." Our experience differs from this forlorn and negative attitude. The young people at the Lollard Adventure Playground properly regard it as theirs, for by their labours they have helped to create it. They have, for instance, built their own workshop and equipped it with workmanlike benches and tools. They have created gardens out of rubble that give pleasure to themselves and to the neighbourhood ; they have constructed a splendid sand pit for the younger children ; they have prepared the ground and laid three thousand turves to make the barren bombed site more attractive, to have a pleasant place for camping, and idle gossip in sunny weather.

In the larger communal hut there is warmth and light during the hours of darkness (when most playgrounds are closed and when young people most need a place to gather). Here they feel at home and are free to paint, to model with clay, to prepare their magazine which is published once a year, to play games, to jive, to act and sing or to read quietly by

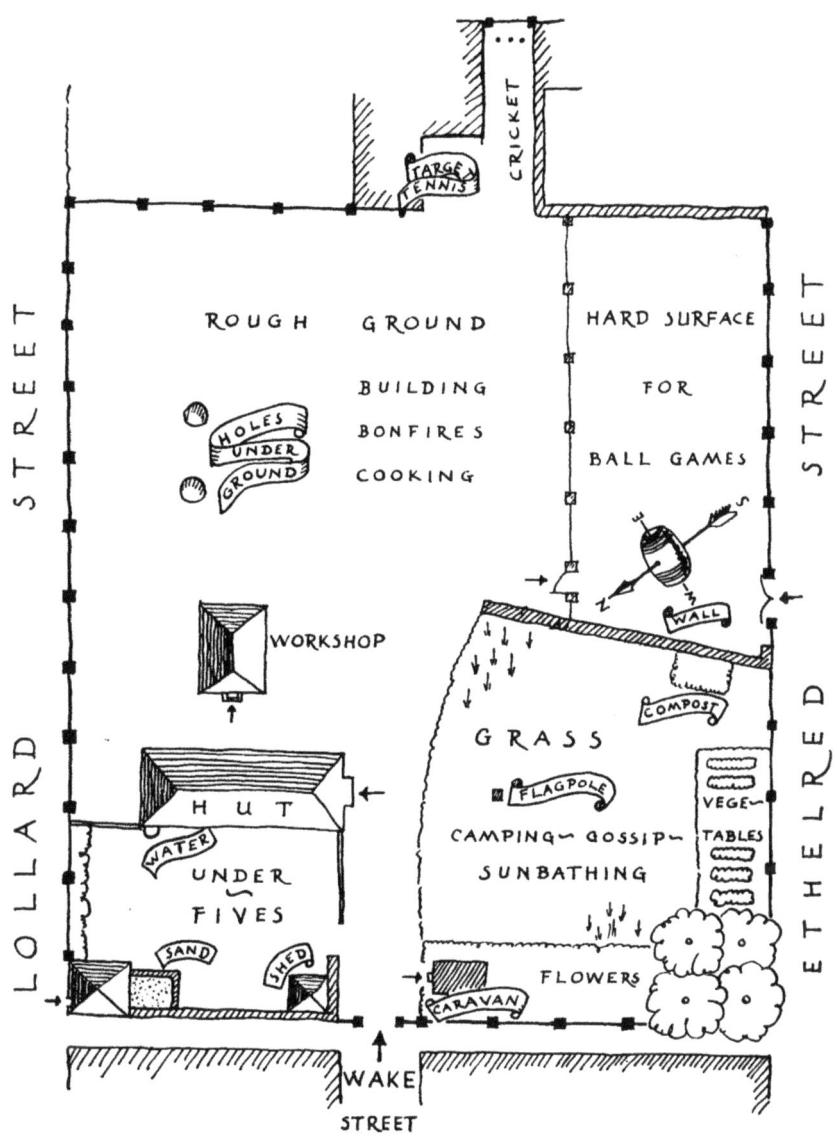

the fire a book from their own library.

Some of these young people come from broken homes and some of them have a very hard struggle to maintain their self-esteem. In common with other growing children they are unconsciously searching for some way to prove to themselves that they have a value and a place in society and they look for a clear road. For instance, the older boys at the Playground, after they had built their workshop, called upon some of the lonely old people in Lambeth and offered to decorate their rooms by papering the walls, painting the ceilings and taking back to their workshop furniture needing repair. It is their pride to do this work at no cost to the Old Age Pensioners and each makes a voluntary contribution from his wage packet towards the cost of materials. They also contribute to the cost of heating and lighting this workshop. Some sixty jobs have been completed in this way in an atmosphere of energy and achievement. They have built a bridge between themselves and the old people and by being protective to those weaker than themselves they identify themselves with the society in which they live. " They are lovely boys " said one old lady but, in fact, they were no different from those who appear to be presenting so many problems today.

Young people wish to have the satisfaction of running their own affairs and, as far as possible, to finance them. Above all, they look for an adult with time, patience and experience with whom they can talk over their perplexities. The popular song from *West Side Story*, " Take my hand and we're half way there," is poignantly true.

As in all aspects of life, fashions come and go at the Lollard Adventure Playground. There is infinite flexibility. Now a gay group of girls enjoy the art of make-up and hairdressing. They, like the boys, have formed their own committee to see how they can give service to the old people. Already some of them undertake weekly shopping for the elderly housebound, others take an old lady for a breather in her wheeled chair and they are seeking other opportunities to help. They are anxious, like the boys, to have some place of their own, perhaps a pre-fabricated hut or an old railway carriage where they can do their cooking, entertain visitors and have pride of possession. They already run a canteen, buy their requirements, keep the necessary books and hope to make a profit. Both the boys' committee and the girls' committee have their own Post Office account.

This playground is different because it's a place where the children have an infinite choice of opportunities. They can handle basic things—earth, water, plants, timber—and work with real tools ; and they have an adult friend, a person they trust and respect. Here every child can develop a healthy sense of self-esteem, because there is always something at which they can excel. The wide age range, from two years to twenty-three, is perhaps unique on any playground. There can be progressive development through rich play opportunities, to a growing sense of responsibility to the playground, to younger children and, finally, to others outside the playground. Their willingness to help others is the sign of real maturity which is the object of all who work with young people.

THE GRIMSBY ADVENTURE PLAYGROUND

'FORT SHANTY, the toddlers' den, built in 1958.'

This playground has been described variously as "a junk heap," "Paradise," "an eyesore," "a kid's kingdom," "a mud dump," "a boon" and "a scandal."

It has been said of it at different times that it is "a wonderful idea," "a nuisance," that it provides "lessons in vandalism" and that it "could be the answer to Britain's problem children."

Before starting on any account of this playground it is necessary to describe, however briefly, its geographical and social setting. Situated on the edge of the timber docks, it is flanked on two sides by a timber yard and a paper mill. Beyond these lie railway sidings and the docks themselves. Facing the playground, and in the streets immediately adjacent, are tiny red brick houses fronting directly on to the pavements. At the back, a network of alleyways links the houses together. One block away, and separated by a main road, is a conventional playground with the usual swings and roundabouts and an open grass pitch. A quarter of a mile away, at the far end of Armstrong Street in which the playground is situated, lies open country.

The houses themselves are occupied by large families (10, 12, 16 or more children), the working members of which are employed mainly on the docks. The fathers are often away at sea, the older children, and sometimes the mothers too, tend to find employment in the fish houses. The social conditions of these families are very mixed, and it is impossible, within the limits of this article, to deal objectively with them.

The children's favourite playgrounds, when not climbing trees or lighting fires on the edge of town, were the streets, back alleys and the dock banks, wherein they found and made their own adventures.

It was with this in mind that the Grimsby Adventure Playground Association was formed. First discussed as an idea by a small group of Grimsby citizens in 1954, and later in correspondence with the National Playing Fields Association, it very soon became possible to hold a public meeting and exhibition. Lady Allen of Hurtwood was invited to be principal speaker, and on the formation of the Association agreed to become its President.

FIRST STEPS

With the Association formed, the real work was about to begin. Where could a playground be found, and at what cost? Here, perhaps, the Association was to receive its first real evidence of the public spirit and interest of the townspeople, industrial concerns and Local Authority departments. An offer of a disused horse paddock of approximately ¾ acre was made by a firm of timber importers, on a lease of five years—and at no cost to the Association. The Parks Committee offered the loan of a tool shed, while an appeal to the N.P.F.A. resulted in a grant to cover the cost of fencing the site. While the Association was busy raising money by means of garden parties and direct appeals, an approach was also made to the Local Education Authority, which agreed to pay the salary of a leader for an experimental period of six weeks.

On the 25th July, 1955, the playground was opened for the first time. Fortunately, the importance of materials had been foreseen, and good quantities of timber, plywood and iron sheeting were available. A fully illustrated account of the experiment subsequently appeared in *The Times Educational Supplement* of 20th April, 1956, and created widespread interest.

' Housing is no problem at Grimsby '

SHANTY TOWN

The constructive abilities and the enterprise shown by the children surprised even those closely concerned with the experiment. The dens, built from old fish boxes, scrap timber and corrugated iron, grew steadily better, and with their development came an awakening of community spirit in the children which, today, has spread beyond the boundaries of the playground itself, into the houses around it.

At first, the dens were not dissimilar from those built by children throughout the ages. As more and more material began to arrive, however, the dens began to assume shapes and characters of their own. One became a hospital, another the fire department ; a hotel was seen, a puppet theatre and a police station, as well as many " private residences " such as *Chez Nous* and — *Bug Hole* . . . .

Shanty Town (the name was the children's own choice) had arrived. Its older citizens in the age range of 10/14 years soon began to embark on projects for the younger members of the community. A special den, with front and back doors, window, neat porch and fence, was built for the under-fives, and later a small sandpit was completed for the same group.

At the start of the experiment, the children had elected a committee, and one of its first decisions was to launch a collection each day so that nails could be bought when needed. At the end of the six weeks holiday, they had collected some £5, and it was fitting, perhaps, that with the closing of the playground, they should decide that a balance of £1 still in hand should be given to the " big committee " (as one lad referred to the Association) " for next year."

At this stage, local opinion was very divided. *The Grimsby Evening Telegraph*, while refraining from any comment itself, gave over much of its correspondence column to letters from " Disgusted Tenant," " Satisfied Owner," " Two Grateful Mothers," " Disgusted Observer," and others who described the playground alternatively as " a social service " and " the most stupid thing that could have happened."

" WE'RE NOT CLOSING "

The return to school was the signal for yet further efforts on the part of the Association. An immediate approach to the L.E.A. resulted in the promise of a grant of 50% towards the leader's salary, should the playground re-open on a full-time basis. The N.P.F.A., too, was eager to help further the scheme, and a grant was made to cover the cost of four brick toilets.

The real problem, however, was still to be overcome. If the playground was to be used throughout the year, it would be necessary to provide indoor facilities for the winter evenings. Although local appeals brought in some response, it soon became evident that this would go only a little way toward meeting the Association's real needs. Appeals were therefore launched over a wider area, and in due course we were very fortunate to gain the interest of the Nuffield Foundation. In July 1956, the Foundation made a generous grant to cover the cost of a hut 40' × 20', complete with heating, lighting and equipment.

Meanwhile, the playground had re-opened for the summer holidays, and it was soon seen that, given adequate supplies of materials, the pattern of play and activities would repeat itself. The cry for more nails was a constant one, and dens continued to surprise by their excellence. Two and three-storey affairs were not uncommon. That year, too, we saw our first " television " (made from an old fish box and car headlamp), a real oven for baking everything from potatoes to clay bricks, and, inevitably, *H.M.S. Sea Shanty* for the toddlers.

At the same time, critics of the scheme had been no less active, and *The Grimsby Evening Telegraph* once again reflected local opinion. "This is a scandal" roared one headline; "Foremost experiment" countered another. One resident opposite the playground threatened to go to the Ministry of Health, while 56 others signed a petition to the Town Council asking that it be closed. A counter petition organised by the mother of two boys using the playground resulted in 232 signatures. Twice the matter came before the Town Council, but each time the decision reached was favourable to the Association.

As the summer neared its end, and preparations were being made for the return to school, the children's cry for nails was replaced by a jubilant "We're not closing" that echoed round the field as they each and separately confirmed that they could still come each evening after school.

THE FIRST WINTER

Although the hut itself was not ready for occupation until January 1957, the children were full of schemes and plans for its use. "Let's have real things," said one lad. "Workbenches," added another, while the girls, determined not to be left out, modestly asked for a sewing machine. All agreed they must have a real shop to make "tea and things." In the event, these were provided—to be used and controlled by the children.

The winter months from January to April proved extremely lively— not to say hectic, with concerts (put on without rehearsal and often with only one day's notice), to raise money for the Nail Fund, an active canteen, with milk, tea and sugar brought from home, countless models from ships and planes to a cage for a tame mouse, while on the sewing machine bibs and aprons were made at an astonishing rate.

Perhaps the most successful activity, however, was the one connected most closely with life outside the playground. Sawing logs has not hitherto been regarded as "child's play," and carting them around the neighbourhood on barrow, pram or back, week after week, to some twenty old age pensioners, was also in the nature of a major operation. Yet this scheme set the seal on a successful winter—and it was with no little pride that the children recorded a total of more than 170 deliveries in ten weeks— with not a penny taken in payment, "Not even for the Nail Fund," as a ten-year-old put it.

To those who doubted whether such an activity would last—who regarded it, perhaps, as a novelty that would wear off, the children replied during the following winter with a total of 264 sacks in thirteen weeks. Indeed, this figure would have been higher still had there been anything left in the playground to saw up.

For proof, the present winter's efforts have *so far* resulted in 334 deliveries, and the children are still sawing.

THE EXPERIMENT IS CONFIRMED

Activities during the summers of 1957 and 1958 not only continued to follow the pattern of previous years: they did so almost to a time table. Again, we first saw the primitive dens—very much " hole in the ground " affairs—followed by a steady improvement as more material began to arrive. By the third week of the school holidays, the first of the community dens began to appear, and very shortly afterwards we were able to list some twenty establishments. These, in 1957, included a town hall, fire station, estate agent, an inn, a builder and demolition contractor (!), as well as shops and a market stall. In 1958, Shanty Town built its own fun fair. Slides, swings and a ghost train were added to the shops as money raising ventures for the Nail Fund, and the record income for one week (16/3d. in 1957) was shattered on three separate occasions. In fact, the total for the six week holiday period of 1958 amounted to £5. 3s. 2d., as against £3. 9s. 8d. in 1957.

The shop, too, has proved itself. It is so much the children's that they even interview the travellers, inspect the samples and place their own orders. Indeed, they have now taken to visiting the warehouse itself " because he's got more things you can see."

In the year 1957, they did a turnover of some £75, reaping a net profit of £10 which was duly donated to the Nail Fund.

During the same period, more direct efforts on behalf of the Nail Fund resulted in a total of more than £25 — which now, of course, provides not only nails, but cottons, chalks, paints and brushes, pencils, scissors, etc.

IN PASSING

While the playground was not established for any particular type of child, it has proved itself most popular with those children who are reluctant to fit into the formal clubs, or who, having tried them, have found themselves at odds with the organised programmes.

Such programmes as there are in Shanty Town are due entirely to the imagination and enterprise of the children themselves. Having thought of an idea, they are encouraged to work towards its fulfilment ; sometimes they fail, but more often than not they succeed. (At the time of writing, the two most recent examples are a football team that failed, and the successful first appearance of what is hoped will be a monthly magazine). But even where they have succeeded, they are always at liberty to evolve new adventures, and at no time are they expected to continue an activity which no longer holds an interest for them.

Together with this is coupled a social attitude towards others which was first evidenced by the building of a special den for the toddlers, and later by the log deliveries to old age pensioners—both of which are now traditional features of life on the playground, and outside.

Care of tools is the responsibility of the children, and it is to their credit that at the end of 1958 they are still using the same tools purchased originally in 1955. Not one hammer or spade has been lost, and all repairs have been paid for out of the Nail Fund.

The hut, too, is their responsibility, and the fact that it is appreciated is evidenced by the care they have taken of it. During the summer months of 1957, when den building was at its most exciting, they took time off to creosote the outside, paint the window frames and put three coats of paint on the interior. This work proved to be a major operation, and for some time a group of working lads stayed on until 10 o'clock at night so that it could be completed before the winter set in. And it is no small tribute to these children when we can record that in our 20 months occupation of the hut, the leader has not yet had to sweep the floor, nor even to ask for volunteers.

MORE FACTS AND FIGURES

TURNOVER. The playground now has a turnover of some 400 or more children, whose ages range from 1-16. It is used, however, mainly by children within the 8-14 age group.

ATTENDANCE. Peak hour attendance figures during the summer have passed the 100 mark, but average around 80. Winter figures, when activities are restricted to the smaller space of the hut, are approximately half this number.

HOURS OF OPENING. *Holidays.*   Mon. to Fri.   10.00 a.m. to 12.30 p.m.
                                                       2.00 p.m. to   5.00 p.m.
                                                       6.00 p.m. to   8.00 p.m.
                                Saturday   10.00 a.m. to 12.30 p.m.
Term Time.   Mon. to Fri.   4.00 p.m. to   8.00 p.m.
                            Saturday   10.00 a.m. to 12.30 p.m.

The playground is not open Saturday afternoons, Sundays and Bank Holidays.

ACCIDENTS. Minor cuts and scratches galore — but no serious accidents of any kind have occurred. First aid dressings are supplied by courtesy of the Nail Fund.

INSURANCE. The children and leader are covered by a comprehensive insurance policy while on the playground, and the children are covered by an additional clause protecting them while engaged on unsupervised activities connected with but outside the playground, i.e., delivering logs to O.A.Ps.

JUVENILE DELINQUENCY. With no official figures available, we can only say, on this point, that a number of our children have been to the Remand Home, both before and since the playground opened. We believe that some may go yet again. We also believe that they will go there much more often if they are prevented from enjoying the adventures that attract them to the playground.

In October 1956, the then Chief of the Grimsby Fire Department allowed himself to be quoted as saying that the area in which the playground is situated was considered a dangerous one, as the children lit fires on the streets and caused accidents. He added that " since the playground has been open the Fire Department's chart for that area has been a blank," and this has been attributed largely to our work on the playground.

LOCAL INHABITANTS. In August 1957, a total of over 300 children and parents set off for a day in Skegness. The money for this outing was raised entirely by the Parents' Group itself, and could not have been achieved but for the goodwill of the neighbourhood. In addition to free sweets, chocolates and crisps, each child was given four shillings pocket money.

In August 1958, the second annual outing took place, with a total of nearly 350 children and parents, who set off similarly in eight coaches. This time, each child was presented with eight shillings pocket money.

While the playground continues to be a source of controversy in the locality—as, for instance, when a "feather storm" invaded nearby houses—the fiercest battles, perhaps, have taken place in the Council Chamber. The Association is fortunate to enjoy the support of the L.E.A. (at present making a grant of 50% of leader's salary), but the fight has by no means proved easy—nor is it proving so today.

Meanwhile, however, while the Association continues to raise money by social functions and direct appeals, the Parents' Group has established itself as a regular and independent "provider." Fortnightly beetle drives, seasonal jumble sales and a Christmas Fair resulted in a sum of more than £70 being donated to the Association during the current twelve months. In addition to this, the Group has raised £20 for its own purposes, such as advertising, prizes, materials for sale of work, etc.

PROBLEMS, PAST AND PRESENT, AND ASPIRATIONS

1. The first problem facing the Association is concerned with its very existence. The scheme costs £800 annually, of which, at the moment, £300 is provided by the L.E.A. The balance of £500 (£300 towards the leader's salary and £200 running costs) left to be found by the Association is a real and recurring broblem.

2. The importance of materials cannot be over-emphasised. Without them the playground becomes pointless as a centre of activity and the children will soon be back on the streets. Organising materials is the leader's responsibility and can prove a full time job on its own. Main supplies are obtained from builders, demolition contractors, ship repairers, box makers and scrap merchants.

3. Major criticisms of the scheme still centre around the playground's "unsightliness." The Association believes this could be largely overcome by the provision of an "eye-proof" fence just inside the existing and otherwise adequate 6' chain mesh.

4. Destructiveness is another charge often levelled at the playground. Here, too, the Association is of the opinion that this arises more through the appearance of the playground itself (which often certainly resembles a battleground) than through fact. "Wrecking" is certainly enjoyed—but is just as certainly restricted by well established and understood rules, reference to which is made at the end of this article.

modern boys' school have been and are of practical assistance (sharpening tools, making the shop counter, etc.), it has been the Association's on occasions, and the Headmaster and staff of the nearby secondary experience that voluntary help is not forthcoming. It is essential that this fact, which the Association believes to be general throughout the country, be recognised—particularly if the children are to be given opportunities to develop their activities.

6. Continuity is yet another problem that has not yet been satisfactorily overcome. The employment of only one leader necessitates closing the playground when he is on holiday, or is absent for any other reason. Further, the employment of an assistant would enable an even greater variety of activities to take place—and would mean real supervision when both the hut and the playground are in use at the same time.

PRINCIPLES

In the struggle to survive, we are often compelled to put first things last. It is reasonable, therefore, that as this article comes to an end we should discuss principles.

For thousands of years, children have argued the case for adventure playgrounds. They have lit fires, built dens, dug holes, crawled into caves, splashed in water—and said " Look, isn't this fun? " For almost as long, adults have either closed their eyes to these activities or, worse, made them punishable offences—crying " No, you must not do that."

But the war between the generations is coming to an end, and we, for our part, are glad to give the victory to the children. Victory in this case, however, does not mean the triumph of one section of the community over another, but an honest and peaceful co-existence based on mutual respect. It means a place where children of all ages can follow their own interests in complete safety, under the eye of an experienced adult : it means a place where children are taught the care and use of tools, where social attitudes towards each other, as well as towards other sections of the community, are encouraged. Above all, it means a place where learning comes naturally with playing.

(There are no written rules in Shanty Town. Rules are repeated by word of mouth, and are now so well established that it is quite common to hear an eight-year-old tell a seven-year-old that he " can't have a fire because there's washing up " on a nearby clothes line.

Similarly, we try to avoid the don'ts so often heard in the adult controlled world. Examples :

(*from any newcomer*) " Can we pull a den down? "
" Yes, providing you've built it yourself."
(*from any regular*) " Can we have tools out? "
" Yes, as soon as you find the missing hammer.")

ADVENTURE PLAYGROUNDS IN ROMFORD

CLOCKHOUSE LANE ADVENTURE PLAYGROUND
showing the second or centre section of the Playground and the first section in the distance

There are two adventure playgrounds in the Borough of Romford. The first, which was opened on 12th November, 1955, is at Clockhouse Lane, Collier Row, in a central position in a primarily residential area at North Romford. The second, opened on 13th April, 1957, is at St. Neots Road, Harold Hill—at the southern end of a large estate developed since the war by the London County Council.

The Parks Committee first gave consideration to the construction of a children's playground at Clockhouse Lane in the latter part of 1953. when the Essex County Council enquired if the Borough Council had any temporary use for a small area of land which had been acquired for the development of a Community Centre at some future date.

Various ideas were considered and negotiations continued with the County Council for several months. The Chairman of the Parks Committee and other members visited " junk " playgrounds in other districts, and gradually there developed the idea of an " adventure " playground where there would be something for all children.

Following the success of the first playground the Parks Committee soon authorised the construction of the second playground at St. Neots Road. Financial assistance was provided by the Essex County Council and the National Playing Fields Association towards the cost of this latter project.

Each playground is controlled, directed and led by a female playground leader under the supervision of the Parks Superintendent and the overall control of the Borough Engineer and Surveyor. The capital cost of the two playgrounds (including equipment installed after the official opening of the sites and before deducting the grants mentioned above) amounted to £3,500. The capital cost, together with the annual maintenance and running costs (approximately £2,000 per annum for the two sites) is met from the Borough Council's General Rate Fund, sponsored by the Parks Committee.

The Clockhouse Lane site is leased from the Essex County Council. and the St. Neots Road site is upon land about to be purchased for open space purposes from the London County Council.

The area of each playground is about 1·2 acres. The Clockhouse Lane site is roughly rectangular having a frontage of about 425 feet and an average depth of about 130 feet. This enabled the site to be divided into three roughly equal areas by chain link fencing.

The first section is intended for very young children, usually accompanied by adults. The grass is kept well trimmed for children's play, but no equipment is provided except a number of park seats. It is found that this area is also appreciated by old people who rest a while here after buying their groceries at the neighbouring shops.

The second section has been provided with a number of items of equipment, some of an unorthodox nature. These are as follows:—

    3 concrete sewer tubes
    Jungle-gym
    Concrete climbing blocks
    2 unserviceable tractors
    Climbing net and frame
    Outdoor gymnastic set
    Unserviceable steamroller
    30 ft. ship's lifeboat.

The section has proved to be very popular. The tractors, the steamroller and the lifeboat were donated free of charge and transported to the site by the Borough Council. All moving parts which were likely to be dangerous to children were removed but the steering wheels and other controls were retained to add realism to the children's play. The vehicles and the boat were bedded in concrete and other items of equipment surrounded by small sandpits.

The third section is the "adventure" section and the only equipment provided is a small hut (about 10′ × 6′) for the leader plus tools, etc., for the use of the children. The children themselves have constructed a small cycle speedway track in this section.

The division of the site into these three sections was experimental but has been successful. The leader is quite definite in her view that the partition fencing is advantageous.

The St. Neots Road Playground is of a different shape being roughly a square and no partition fencing was provided. The playground equipment was, however, concentrated at the northern end of the site, the southern end of the site left clear as a play area, with a few seats, and the central area intended for activities of the "adventure" category.

The playground equipment comprises:—

    Outdoor gymnastic set
    Climbing net and frame
    Jungle-gym
    3 concrete sewer tubes
    Unserviceable tractor
    Concrete climbing blocks
    Horizontal ladder
    Sandpit
    30 ft. ship's lifeboat
    Set of 6 cradle swings
    Set of 4 10 ft. swings.

(The two sets of swings have been installed since the site was opened in response to a demand from the children for this type of equipment).

Recently an additional area of about $1\frac{1}{4}$ acres adjacent to this playground has been made available to the leader for organised games.

The sites are normally open on weekdays (except Mondays) from 11 a.m. until the appropriate park closing time depending upon the season of the year, but are opened an hour earlier during school holidays. On Sundays the opening times are from 9.30 a.m. until 1.30 p.m. The sites are closed on Mondays (leader's day off) except during school holidays.

A census was taken during the latter half of 1958 of the number of children attending the playgrounds. During a typical week in July, while children were still at school, the average figures for Clockhouse Lane were (a) before 1 p.m.—27, (b) 1 p.m.-4 p.m.—53, (c) after 4 p.m.—50. During the second week of the summer holidays these figures increased to 84, 140 and 141 respectively. The figures for the St. Neots Road site have generally been about 50% above those for Clockhouse Lane, due largely to its situation upon a new housing estate with a dearth of equipped playgrounds (a matter which is now receiving attention). Attendances do, of course, fall off during winter months.

The Clockhouse Lane playground provides an incidental service during school terms, since it enables parents to leave young children 3 to 5 years of age for half-an-hour or so in the morning and afternoon while they visit the nearby shops. As the numbers at the playground at these times are relatively small the leader is able to give the "toddlers" personal attention. Some items of kindergarten equipment have now been purchased for use at this and at the St. Neots Road site.

With the many and varied activities and the high numbers of children attending the playgrounds it is probably inevitable that some accidents will occur. The adventure playgrounds do not, however, compare unfavourably with the orthodox equipped playgrounds in the parks. The injuries that do occur are largely of a superficial nature, abrasions, etc.

The activities of the two playgrounds are numerous and the leaders seek to encourage the children to make suggestions and then assist them to make their own arrangements to implement the suggestions. A feature of the Clockhouse Lane site is the individual gardens maintained by the children. These usually measure about $8' \times 8'$ edged with bricks or concrete by the children. Competitions are held to judge the best kept garden and the results are very good—some children have even grown their own bedding plants from seeds. The children are helped by the supply of a few dozen surplus plants by the Parks Superintendent.

Various pets have been kept at the sites from time to time but this aspect of the playground activities needs very special attention to ensure that the animals live in reasonable conditions and are properly fed. A group of boys at Clockhouse Lane have planned to start a racing pigeon group, others propose to keep budgerigars. In addition the playground pets club meets from time to time ; dogs, hamsters, rabbits, etc., are brought along for an hour and competitions are held including the "dog with the fastest wagging tail" trial, and the like.

There is always something for the children to tackle in the adventure sections of the playgrounds. Ballast, sand, cement, bricks, second-hand timber, etc., are provided by the Borough Engineer and Surveyor. The "projects" upon which they spend their time and energy are limited only by the imagination of the children and their leaders. Tools are also provided by the Borough Engineer and Surveyor—very largely these comprise old shovels, picks, etc., which have worn down to such a size as to be of no value to the Council's Direct Labour Sections.

The leaders of the two sites endeavour to arrange special events to which the children are able to look forward. Both sites elect annually a Playground Queen, complete with attendants, and upon these days there are fêtes, etc., arranged, to some extent, by the children themselves. Similar events are usually held during the Whitsun and Summer holidays with considerable success. The leader at Clockhouse Lane estimates that the attendance at the last fête approached 2,000 and the total takings for the day amounted to £41. Most of the income from these events is used to pay for "outings" to the seaside for regular attenders at the playgrounds, or handed over in cash or kind to help Old Age Pensioners in the neighbourhood.

Both playgrounds usually participate in the annual Romford Carnival procession and fête which is held for charitable causes, and their floats have gained awards. The St. Neots Road playground has also assisted with the Festival of Youth Carnival sponsored by various organisations on the Harold Hill estate.

The indoor activities at the sites are limited by the lack of accommodation. As previously mentioned the leader's hut at Clockhouse Lane measures only 10' × 6' and was originally intended to be used only by her. Although the size was increased to 12' × 10' when the St. Neots Road site was designed it is found that it is still far from adequate. Consideration has been given to the provision of additional play huts and a contract has now been placed for the provision and erection of a sectional pre-cast concrete building at the St. Neots Road site which will include a play area measuring about 22' 0" × 17' 6" and toilet accommodation for boys and girls.

Despite the lack of facilities, however, much work is carried out indoors. At Clockhouse Lane an informal "skiffle" group meets from time to time—the playground leader has passed on the rudiments of the guitar to a number of boys. At St. Neots Road a small choir and a concert group has been formed, which performs at the site's concerts and has also given many performances at various venues on the housing estate. The leader at this site also runs a small tuck shop, in view of the distance to the nearest sweet shop.

The provision of toilet accommodation is an important point which can easily be overlooked. Fortunately at Clockhouse Lane there is a public convenience adjacent to the site, but at St. Neots Road, as a matter of expediency, temporary timber structures containing chemical closets were erected. These have not proved satisfactory and as mentioned above new toilet accommodation is now to be provided.

A very promising development at St. Neots Road has been the introduction of a scheme for helping local old people. About 70 children take part. They are issued with a card by the leader and when they have time to spare they report to her for a task. When the job is done the "beneficiary" initials the card and the boy or girl gains a point. It is planned to award prizes at the end of the year to the children having the highest tally of points.

The Chairman of the Parks Committee takes a personal interest in both sites and pays frequent visits. The present and past Mayors of the Borough have also attended many functions at the sites and have contributed a large measure of encouragement to the leaders and the children.

It would, of course, be impossible for all these activities to be undertaken if the playground leader were dependent upon her own exertions alone. Fortunately a number of parents accompany young children to the sites and thus assist supervision. There is also a good deal of voluntary help given to make the fêtes, etc., the success they are.

It would be foolish to pretend that no complaints are received. To bring hundreds of children to a new playground adjacent to established residential properties is almost bound to meet with some opposition, but it has been found, particularly at Clockhouse Lane, that the criticism tends to diminish after a few months and good neighbourly relations may be established through the tact and diplomacy of a good leader.

It would be a fine thing if it were possible to conclude this paper by quoting dramatic reductions in the incidence of juvenile delinquency and road accidents. The Superintendent of Police agrees that the playgrounds are helpful in keeping the children off the streets but statistics show that the total number of juveniles brought before the Magistrates has been increasing over the last few years. This is no doubt mainly due to the large increase in population, particularly among children, in the same period, but it does make it hazardous to draw any definite conclusions upon this aspect.

THE RATHBONE STREET ADVENTURE

PLAYGROUND, LIVERPOOL

At an inaugural meeting held in 1950 of local clergy, headmasters, police and social workers, the Pitt Street and Area Juvenile Committee was formed. Its aims were to take active steps to ensure the welfare of the children in the area, with special reference to the problem of Juvenile Delinquency. This part of Liverpool, though fairly near the centre of the city and subject to much rebuilding and redevelopment, has certain areas that are very depressed. It is also perhaps the most racially mixed section of any English city.

The Committee immediately resolved to find a playing space. Within a year a suitable site had been found, though it was realised that the site would not be permanent. Responsibility for supervision and organisation was accepted by the committee while the University Settlement, where it met, and whose Warden was Chairman, agreed to act as the centre of activities.

With the support of the Local Authority the site was gradually prepared, equipment was assembled and local support solicited. By the beginning of 1954 it was possible to appoint a leader. Initially a grant for the leader's salary was most generously provided by the N.P.F.A., but more recently this has been replaced by a direct grant from the local Education Authority. Administrative matters have always been dealt with by the Settlement and the leader's salary has been supplemented so that some other work could be undertaken by him.

The playground is divided into three areas of about the same size. One, which is adjacent to the street and not enclosed, contains items of conventional equipment—a swing, merry-go-round, slide, see-saw and sandpit. This is without doubt the most used section as much, perhaps, because of its accessibility as for its attractions. It is used all day and often, in the evenings, by teen-age boys and girls as a rendezvous. Considering that the equipment is never locked relatively little damage has been suffered. This section is not surfaced. The sandpit was formerly a ship's lifeboat containing sand, but this was recently replaced with a specially designed concrete structure with two end walls supporting a bouncing plank of pre-stressed concrete and with a sewer pipe let through each wall to form a tunnel.

The second section of the playground is a sports pitch with a surface of rolled granite chips. Tubular goal posts are provided, but the area is used for other games besides football. Though fenced on one side it, too, is readily accessible and is used by playground children, schools and groups of local youths.

The Adventure section is completely enclosed by a wire fence and has a gateway large enough to allow a lorry to enter. This section is unsurfaced. It contains old vans, car bodies, lifeboats, rollers, a petrol pump and several concrete structures. There are tools available for digging, but this is very tough going since the site is solid with bricks (it is a former blitzed area). A small hut, originally intended for storage, has recently had an interior partition provided, thus enabling the larger part to be used for activities. These range from light crafts to stamp collecting. An experiment this year has been to provide a Baby Corner. Based round seats for the mothers it comprised equipment such as a small swing, rocking horse, blackboards and large tin baths for water play. Only children under the age of six were permitted. Older boys and girls helped to supervise.

The playground is open from 9 a.m. till sunset in Winter and until 9 or 10 p.m. in Summer. Two part-time caretakers supervise the site when the leader is absent. Numbers of children using the playground vary considerably. A handful seem always to be there regardless of the weather but on a fine day in Summer over 150 children will be present at a time.

Accidents have been confined mainly to cuts and bruises and a fractured arm is the most serious accident in the playground's history. The routine for dealing with accidents is well known to the children, who report to the Leader or Caretaker.

The principle on which the playground has been organised during the present leadership is that of providing the children with a place where they can indulge in all sorts of play with the minimum of adult interference. In many things the children need guidance ; if older children create a situation which is dangerous to younger ones the leader must obviously become involved. To solve such difficulties the Playground Patrol was formed. It is now about 60 strong and consists of local children who use the playground really regularly. Senior children graduate by conduct and character into Patrol Leaders and Committee members. This scheme has done much to foster a loyalty to the playground as a small community.

The relationship of the playground to outside authorities is good. Much free material has been supplied by firms, on request, and help has often been obtained from such City authorities as the Surveyor and Engineer's Department, Parks and Gardens, etc. Parents, Police and local Heads of schools are most co-operative.

Although the site is hemmed in by busy main roads, road accidents are negligible. This is the more remarkable because there are motor cycle repair shops nearby and the area is also used for driving instruction and testing.

Some of the older boys are on probation, and many derelict buildings around the site are a temptation for breaking in and as meeting places for small gangs. Since the link with the Settlement has been so close the transition from Playground to Clubs has been a natural one for many children. Associated with the Settlement are three Boys' Clubs (including a specialised one for difficult and delinquent boys between the ages of

8 and 12), a Girls' Club and a Play Centre. In the immediate future there are plans to extend the work of the Baby Corner by opening a Day Nursery under the supervision of a qualified Matron. This will be housed in premises a few hundred yards from the Playground.

It is difficult to make long-term future plans when the whole future of the playground site is uncertain. Nevertheless, any work on the site is itself useful as an activity and each improvement attempted does something for the feeling of responsibility not only of the children but of the adults as well. Much has been attempted to interest all sections of the community ; the News Sheets and the visits to schools and business firms have played important parts. So too has the support given to us by the visits to the playground of well-known local persons such as Mrs. Bessie Braddock, M.P. There is a need to carry the interest of large firms in the city a stage further so that they will commit themselves to give regular support. And, as always in this sphere of Social Work, the necessity of finding voluntary helpers.

SOUTHMEAD ADVENTURE PLAYGROUND, BRISTOL

'*Enjoying a variety of activities*'

The idea of an adventure playground had long been in the minds of a number of people in Bristol and was further stimulated by a visit from Lady Allen of Hurtwood in May, 1954.

As a result of discussions, the Planning and Public Works Committee felt that this was a matter for the Education Authority. The Education Authority accordingly decided to set up a Playground. The Bristol Social Project was also interested in the scheme. Planning approval was then given for a site on Southmead, a housing estate, half pre-war and half post-war, on the outskirts of Bristol and the Housing Committee agreed that this site be used for an adventure playground for a purely nominal charge.

The site is about one and one-third acres and has been fenced in. One small part has been levelled, but otherwise it includes banks, ditches, and on one side drops down to a stream.

The Playground was opened in May, 1955, under the auspices of an active committee on which the Education Committee, the Housing Committee, the Bristol Social Project and the local Community Council for Southmead were represented. Financial assistance to launch the scheme came from the following sources — the Education Committee made a capital grant, the Housing Committee leased the site and have also assisted with invaluable financial and practical help. The Bristol Social Project undertook to pay £300 for two years towards the salary of £450 of a full time leader who would spend some time making observations for the Project and reporting these to the Director of the Project.

This offer was accepted although some members had misgivings as to what the position would be when the two years were up. A grant was made by the National Playing Fields Association and a building firm made a gift of £500. Other firms and local residents have also assisted with help in various forms. In July, 1955, a hut was erected on the site, with the voluntary help for one month of an international students' camp, supplemented by some voluntary local helpers.

During the first two years the Playground was open every weekday after school hours, but when the Bristol Social Project grant ceased in 1957 a smaller income made it necessary to employ a part-time leader. Numbers attending ranged between 60-100 with an average range of 5-15 years. There have, of course, been the usual cuts and bruises but no serious accidents to date.

Good use is made of the Playground and the children get endless joy digging the ground or attacking tree trunks. Moderate success has been achieved by some limited carpentering efforts, others enjoy building or alternatively demolishing what they built the day before. Construction of dens, particularly for use in winter evenings, from stones, bricks and corrugated iron was most popular over a long period. All ages enjoy the fixed climbing frame and sunken baths provide popular water play for the younger children. The stream is naturally very popular and when there is sufficient water dams are constructed and there is endless play with a boat.

Adequate leadership is of prior importance and it has been very difficult to get such part-time help. This, coupled with the financial problem, meant that the Playground had to be closed for the first part of 1958, but at Whitsuntide it was opened again for two evenings a week. This was made possible by the voluntary help of a loyal and enthusiastic, if small, band of helpers, three Committee members and parents and friends living in the district, who agreed to carry on, pending more permanent arrangement for staffing. At the end of July, with the approval of the Education Committee, a new scheme was put into operation. This was made possible by a further generous grant from the National Playing Fields Association in conjunction with the Bristol Education Committee and the Housing Committee.

'*Fun with the ropes*'

Mr. G. H. Sylvester, Chief Education Officer for Bristol, had been deeply interested from the outset and was most anxious to try a scheme, whereby eight teachers might provide the leadership jointly, working two at a time on a rota, each doing one evening session of three hours per week and 44 weeks in the year, closing during December, January and February. It is too soon to make more than general comments. In a playground of this kind, where the aim is to give children freer opportunities for development of the spirit of adventure and imaginative play, a special type of person is needed to offer judicious advice, help and suggestion, and the individuals of any group will have a varied approach.

The team will therefore meet periodically to discuss difficulties and have some general agreement as to action in certain circumstances.

The scheme is in the main working well. The main problems that have arisen to date are :—
- (1) How best to ensure a steady flow of adequate equipment.
- (2) Distribution and collection of tools.
- (3) How best to deal with groups of older boys who come to disturb rather than to take part in activities.
- (4) What to do about periodic wanton destruction, when the Playground is closed, probably by non-users.
- (5) What to do about thefts of tools and other equipment.

Members of the Committee are well aware of these problems and are doing their best to solve them.

ST. JOHN'S WOOD TERRACE ADVENTURE PLAYGROUND, LONDON

A Christmas Party for the old people given and paid for by the children.

How the Playground Started

The Playground was started at the end of 1956 because a need was expressed by several of the local inhabitants, particularly a caretaker of a block of flats, who was appalled by the number of children of all ages, playing on the streets, throwing stones, and generally appearing to have no central place to play. Concern was also expressed at the amount of street accidents to children, parents often being unable to escort their children over the busy road to the park.

Who Administers and Manages it?

A Committee of local residents was formed, including Lady Allen of Hurtwood, whose advice and experience were invaluable. This Executive Committee is responsible for the administration of the Playground.

In January 1957 an Association of members was formed, the Mayor of Marylebone accepting the position of President, and the Member of Parliament, Sir Wavell Wakefield, accepted the position of Vice-President. The Executive Committee report annually to the Association.

The management of the Playground is administered by a full time Warden, in co-operation with the Executive Committee.

How it is Financed

The Playground is assisted by grants from the National Playing Fields Association and the London and Greater London Playing Fields Association. Also a grant towards the Warden's salary is given by the London County Council.

There are about 400 members of the Association who subscribe varying amounts from 2/6 p.a. to £5 p.a.

Various gifts both from individuals and organisations, e.g., the local Primary School donated the proceeds of their children's annual Play.

Area of Playground

144 ft. by 90 ft., consisting of main tarmac area, grass lawn, flower garden, sand pit, rough play area (digging, fire lighting), centrally heated hut 18 ft. by 30 ft.

When Open

    Term Time — 12.30 p.m. to 2.30 p.m., 4 p.m. to 8 p.m.
                  Saturday 10 a.m. to 8 p.m.
    School Holidays —
                  10 a.m. to 8 p.m. including Saturdays.
Closed at all times on Wednesday and Sunday.

Numbers Attending

Over 250 on the register. Holiday time about 70 daily. The numbers in the Term Time about 50 daily. Numbers in the evening have to be limited because of the size of the hut.

Accidents

Minor casualties (cuts and abrasions). We are fortunate that our Warden has nursing qualifications.

ACTIVITIES
The main activities indoors are: games (chess, draughts, etc.), plasticine, painting, reading, record playing. There are special evenings for drama, musical appreciation, dancing, carpentry, sewing, etc.

The evenings are broken up into periods for the younger members, teen-agers, also various group activities, since the numbers grow all the time, and the space of the hut is limited.

The main activities outdoors are: games of all kinds, both organised and free play; building huts from spare wood, also use of the Swedish blocks which are enormously popular for building and all kinds of imaginative games; digging, making fires, also use of the jumping horse and other equipment; gardening, wall building, etc.

THE PRINCIPLES ON WHICH THE PLAYGROUND IS RUN

To encourage a friendly communal spirit, a sense of ownership and the feeling of responsibility thereby implied. It was felt that in these days of congested built-up areas there was a great need of a safe place to play, which children would feel all their own. A place where children could find scope for constructive, imaginative and educational play, under adult supervision.

It has been found that individual personalities and talents thrive and develop under these conditions.

The presence of a trained Warden, a friend skilled in the understanding of the basic needs of children, is a great asset to the children, who find someone always available to listen to their interest, and sort out their difficulties, emotional and technical.

Parents too are reassured in the knowledge that a trained adult is present and that the children are off the streets, where unguarded and uncontrolled activities are likely to be obstreperous and dangerous to others, rather than constructive and educational to themselves.

RELATIONS WITH OUTSIDE ORGANISATIONS

Guides use the hut from time to time.

A local football team has used the hut for meetings.

Helpful relations obtain with the local Churches, also with the Scouts and the Schools.

ATTITUDE OF LOCAL INHABITANTS, PARENTS AND POLICE

At first the attitude of some local inhabitants was sceptical and apprehensive, but apart from very few minor complaints, we enjoy the utmost co-operation.

Parents are most co-operative both in supporting the Warden and discussing the problems of their individual children. Parents also give their services in various ways from time to time.

Police are most helpful, and it has been interesting that in several cases co-operation between the police and the Warden has assisted with some of the difficult children.

VOLUNTARY HELP

Parents have offered some of their spare time, which has been most useful on many occasions. Various offers have been received for helping with carpentry, watch making, shoe repairing, sewing, etc.

JUVENILE DELINQUENCY

Several excellent results with some of the problem children have been achieved by the co-operation of the police and probation officers, whereby the Warden's privileged position, as friend and in many cases " *confidente* " of the children, has helped to sort out some of the problems.

LOCAL AUTHORITIES

The ground of the playground is leased from the St. Marylebone Council, for a peppercorn rent. There has been an excellent co-operation between the Borough Engineer, who assisted with the fencing, the Borough Treasurer, who is the Hon. Auditor for the Association, the Works Committee who among other things have just donated an excellent lorry to the playground, the Borough Library, and the Parks Superintendent. The Mayor of Marylebone is the President, and Sir Wavell Wakefield, the M.P. for the Borough, the Vice-President of the Association.

Local schools are most helpful, and two members of the staff are on the Executive Committee. The L.C.C. built a fence and gates, and contribute towards the Warden's salary.

TO SUM UP the achievements of the St. John's Wood Adventure Playground in the two years since its inauguration :

The Committee feel that the most important development arising out of this experiment has been the marked change in the attitude of the children and the parents. The children have grown from irresponsible individuals into an organised happy community, willing to accept the advantages and to share in the responsibilities as exemplified in the following :—

1. They have formed Committees which are responsible for the discipline, cleanliness and general running of the activities of the playground.
2. They formed a Committee and raised and saved money to buy a radiogram.
3. They have helped to make their own garden, and cared for it all the summer. They also built a garden wall.
4. Recently a Bazaar and Jumble Sale was organised and run by the children themselves, and part of the money raised was voluntarily donated to the general funds of the Association.
5. The remainder of the money the children are proposing to use for :
    a. their own Christmas festivities ;
    b. a party for old people ;
    c. a return of hospitality to some of the children from the Lollard Street Adventure Playground.

6. The children run a very successful canteen, which is open at all times.

However well intentioned the efforts of the Committee may be, the basic factor for success lies in the personality of the Warden. He is in daily contact with the children, and his fundamental qualification should be a love of children, and an understanding of their psychology. This involves an ability to listen and guide, rather than instruct and direct authoritatively. In such circumstances the children are able to enjoy constructive play, giving expression to their own creative energies.

The St. John's Wood Adventure Playground, now nearing the end of its third year, continues to grow and to enlarge its membership and activities. During 1959 three very important new ventures have been successfully and happily launched.

1. *The Nursery Group.* Ever since the inception of the Playground, we have been requested by mothers to run a group for the " Under fives " since the facilities in the neighbourhood do not cater for a fraction of the small children who wish to go to a nursery school. " Save the Children Fund " have given us the services of an experienced worker to run such a group two half days a week. This project has been a tremendous success, and owing to the limitations of the hut, we have had to refuse further admission for the present, and have a waiting list of over 50 children. The spacious hut is centrally heated, and the children have use of all the moveable equipment and the run of the playground, the Leader being assisted in her supervision by a rota of mothers.

2. *The Parents' Committee.* It was the intention and hope of the Executive Committee that the parents would play a more active part in the running of the playground, and that they would feel that they had much to contribute in the way of interest, time and effort for their own children and those of the neighbourhood. This Committee was formed this year, and is now a most enthusiastic and active body. Their main intention is to help raise money for necessary equipment for the playground and to take over the responsibility of guiding the Teen-Age Group, and finding persons who would be capable of helping with the various interests that may be undertaken.

3. *The Teen-Age Group.* Originally it was the intention of the Executive Committee to cater for children between the ages of approximately 5 to 12 years of age. However, as the playground became more and more popular it was found that children up to 17 years of age were coming to the playground. Owing to the limited size of the hut and the area, it was decided at the end of the summer to revert to the original intention and limit the age group up to the age of 12 years, for the welfare and safety of all. Arising out of this decision, a Teen-Age Group has been formed having their own Committee and rota of parents who supervise. At present this group meets one evening a week, when the younger children have left. The parents and teen-agers hope to build a workshop, so that they may include carpentry, drama and hairdressing to name only a few of the creative activities in addition to their jiving and social efforts.

www.ingramcontent.com/pod-product-compliance
Ingram Content Group UK Ltd.
Pitfield, Milton Keynes, MK11 3LW, UK
UKHW021325180426
11947UKWH00017B/1452